boogie woogie

Arranged by Brent Edstrom

ISBN 978-1-70513-177-0

Visit Hal Leonard Online at
www.halleonard.com

Contact us:
Hal Leonard
7777 West Bluemound Road
Milwaukee, WI 53213
Email: info@halleonard.com

In Europe, contact:
Hal Leonard Europe Limited
42 Wigmore Street
Marylebone, London, W1U 2RN
Email: info@halleonardeurope.com

In Australia, contact:
Hal Leonard Australia Pty. Ltd.
4 Lentara Court
Cheltenham, Victoria, 3192 Australia
Email: info@halleonard.com.au

contents

BARRELHOUSE BREAKDOWN

By PETE JOHNSON

Fast Boogie Woogie

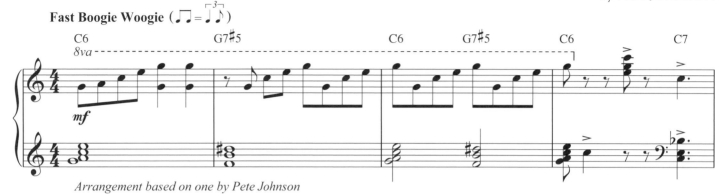

Arrangement based on one by Pete Johnson

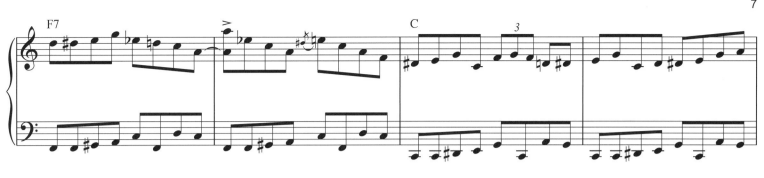

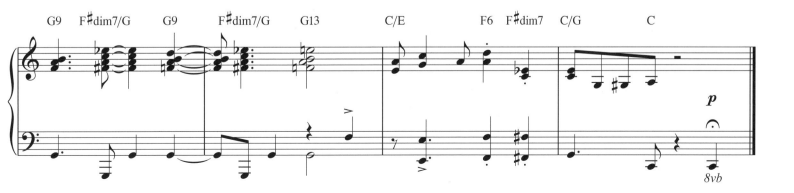

BASS GONE CRAZY

By ALBERT AMMONS

Bright Boogie Woogie, with a very slight lilt

Arrangement based on a performance by Albert Ammons

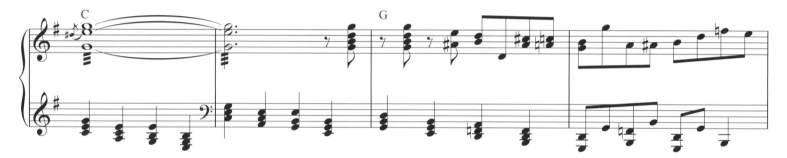

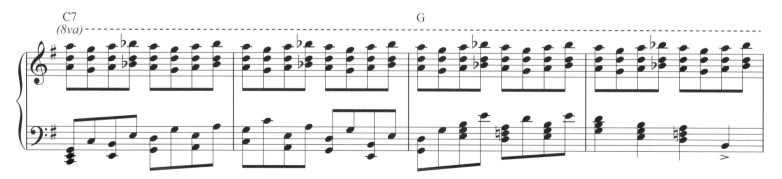

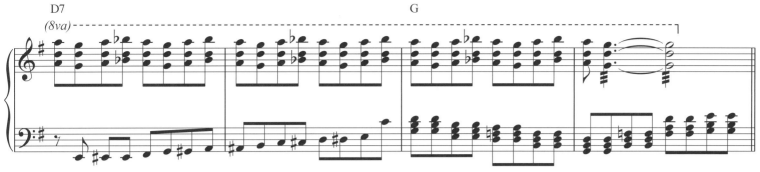

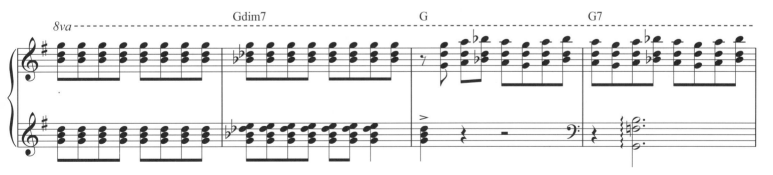

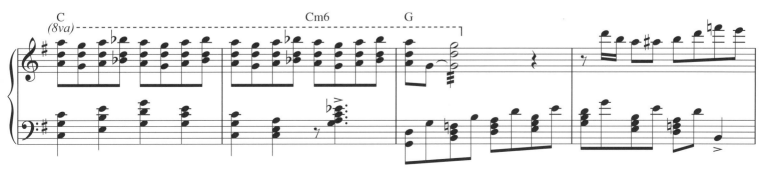

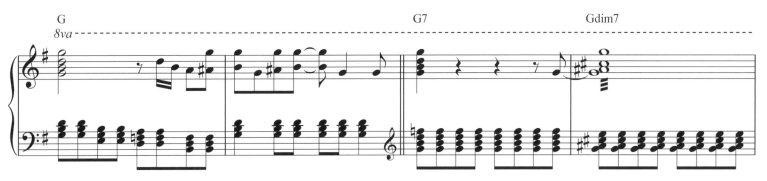

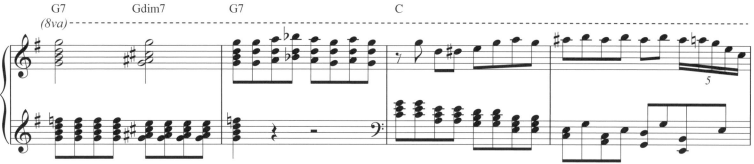

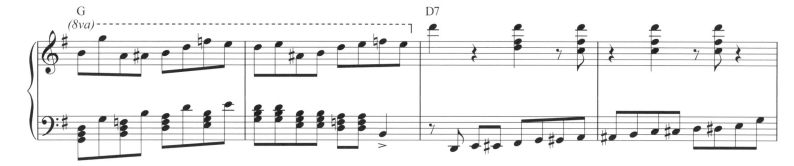

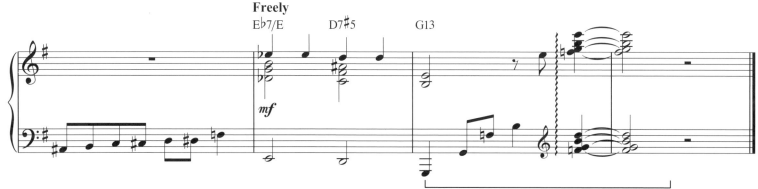

DOWN THE ROAD A PIECE

Words and Music by
DON RAYE

Moderately, straight 8ths

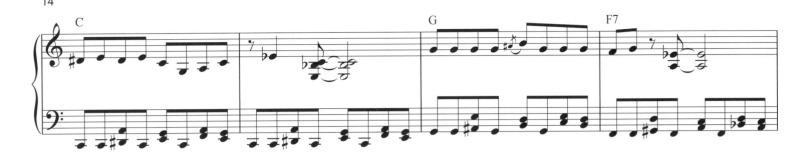

To Coda ⊕

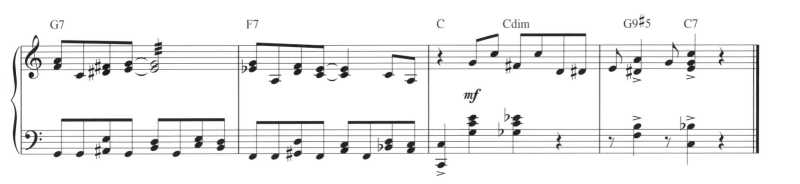

BASS ON TOP

By MEADE "LUX" LEWIS

Arrangement based on a performance by Meade "Lux" Lewis

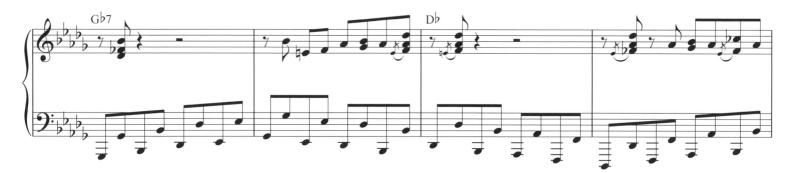

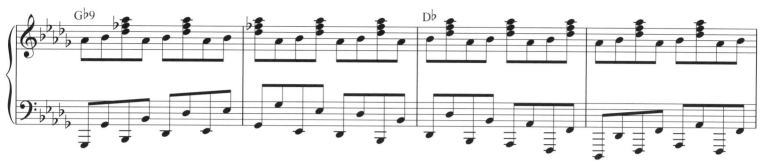

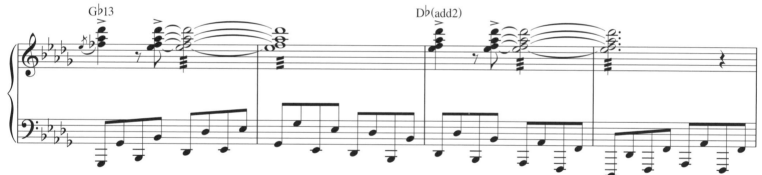

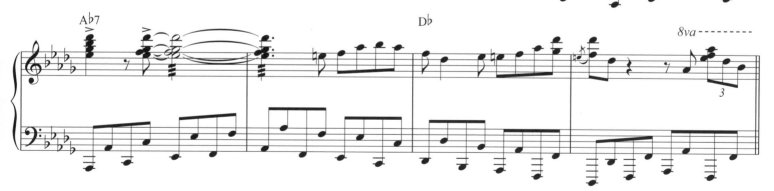

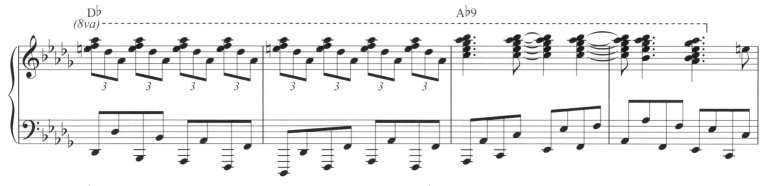

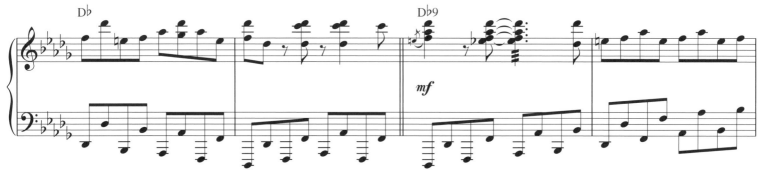

21

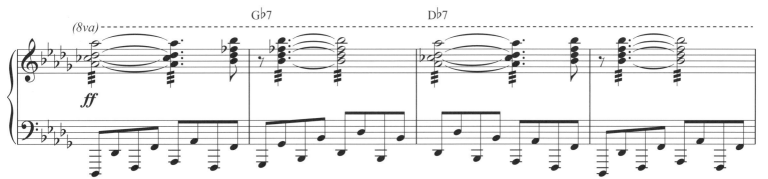

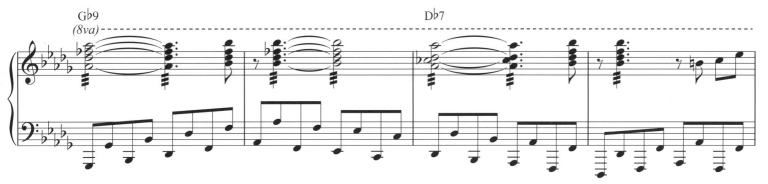

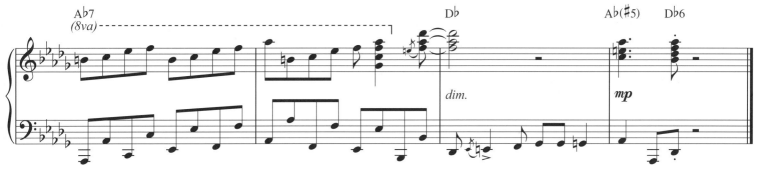

BOOGIE WOOGIE BLUES

By ALBERT AMMONS

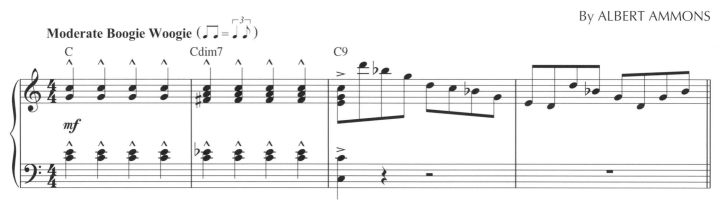

Arrangement based on a performance by Albert Ammons

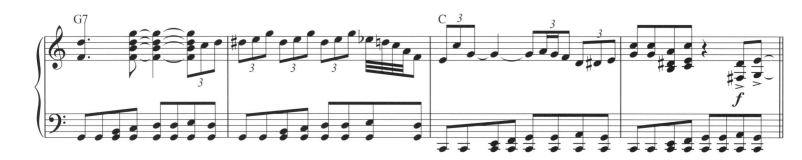

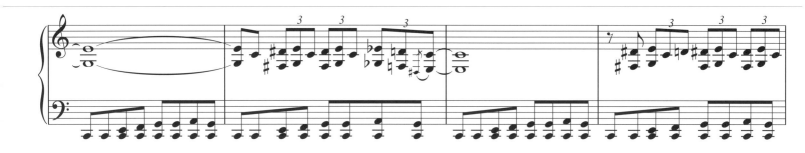

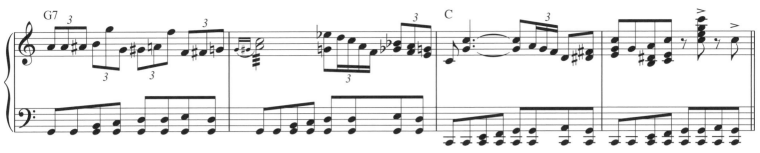

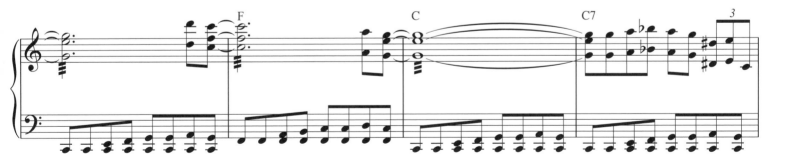
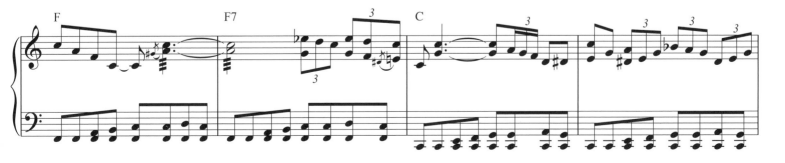

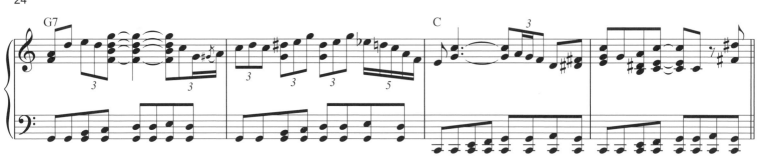

25

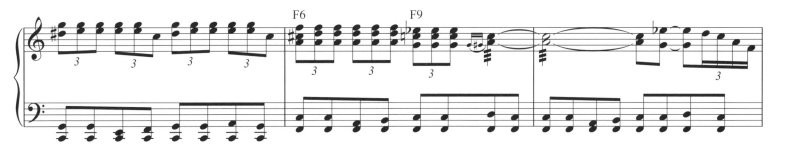

BOOGIE WOOGIE MAN

By ALBERT AMMONS
and PETE JOHNSON

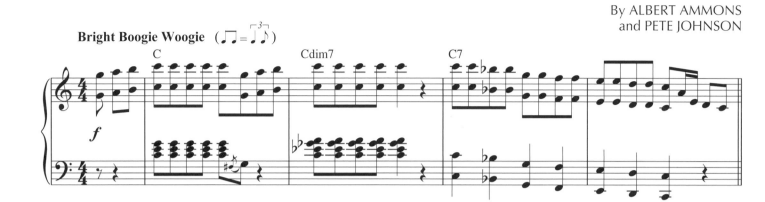

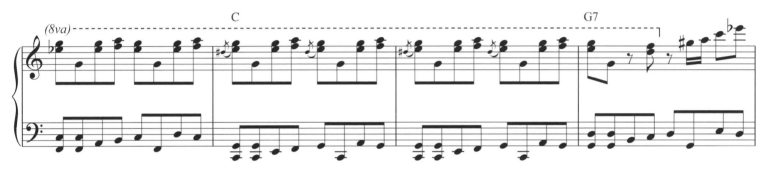

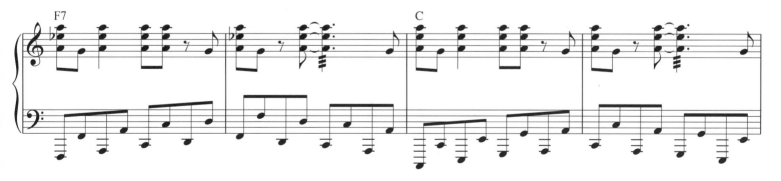

BOOGIE WOOGIE STOMP

By ALBERT AMMONS

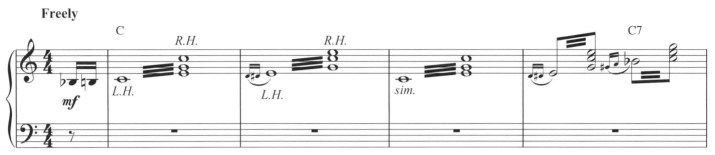

Arrangement based on one by Albert Ammons

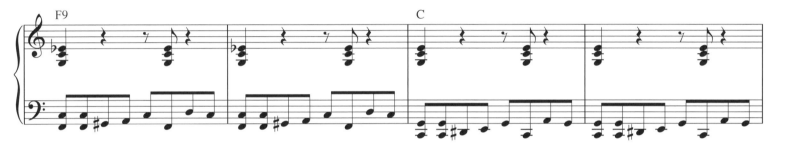

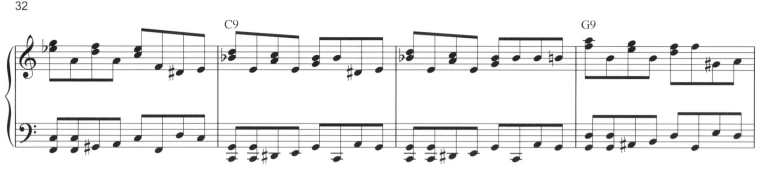

CHICAGO BREAKDOWN

By MACEO MERIWEATHER

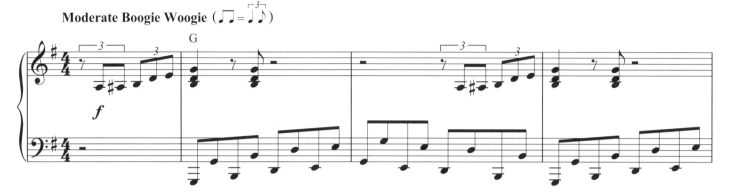

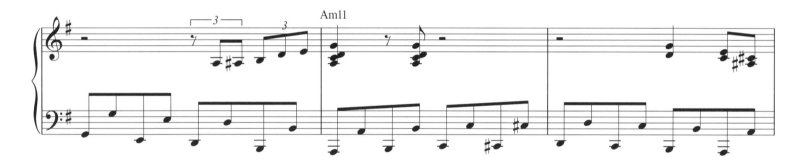

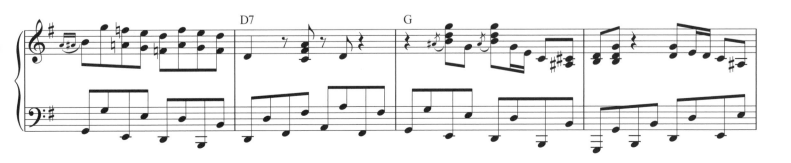

CLIMBIN' AND SCREAMIN'

By PETE JOHNSON

Bright Boogie Woogie

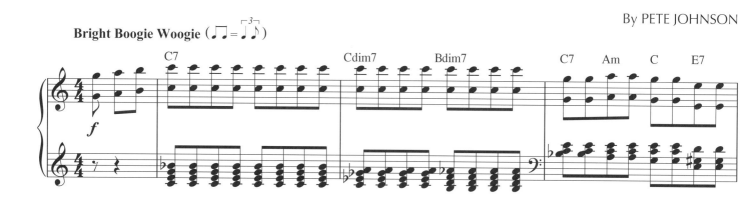

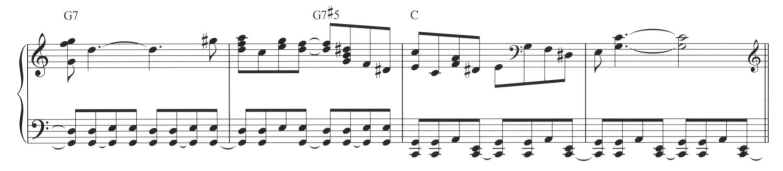

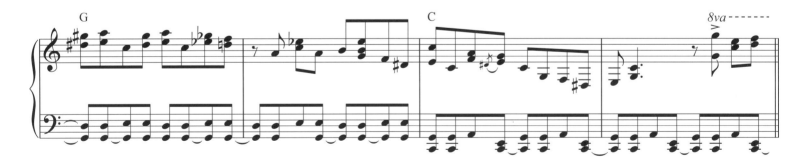

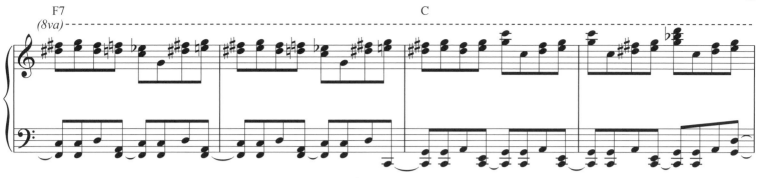

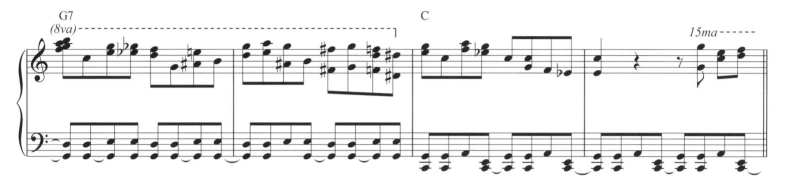

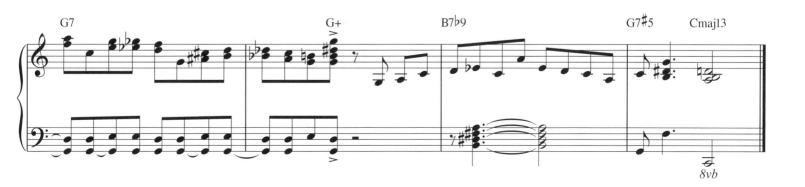

FIVE O'CLOCK BLUES

Words and Music by
JAMES YANCEY

Moderate Swing

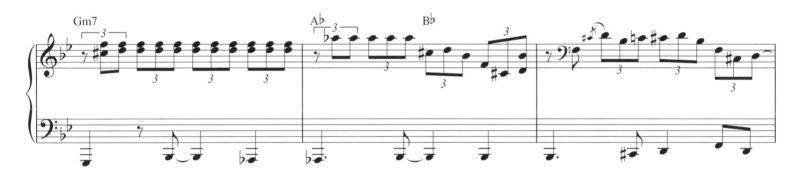

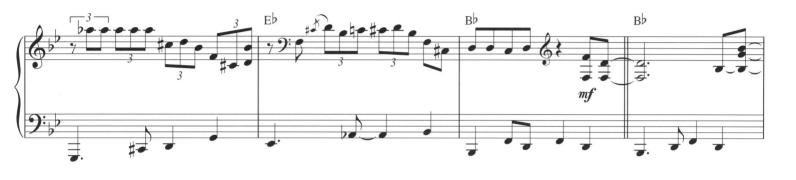

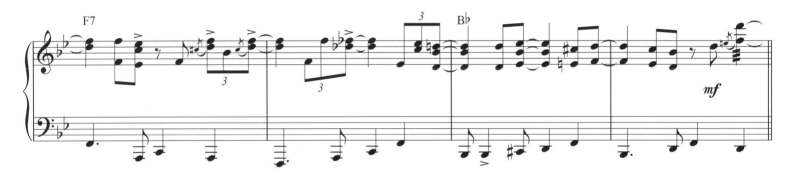

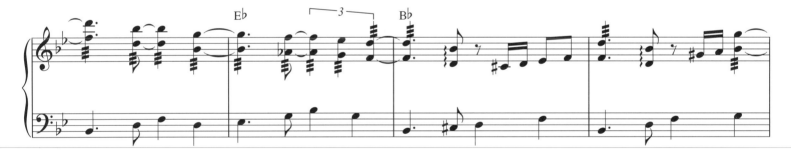

HOLLER, STOMP

By PETE JOHNSON

Fast Boogie Woogie

Arrangement based on a performance by Pete Johnson

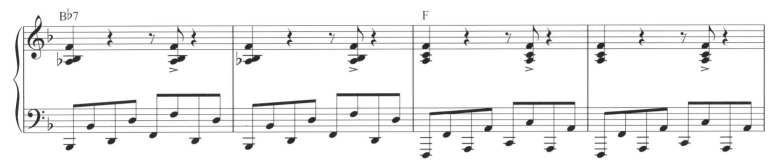

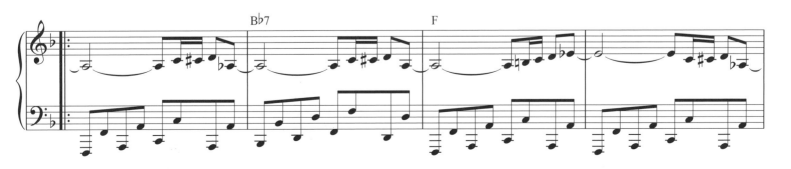

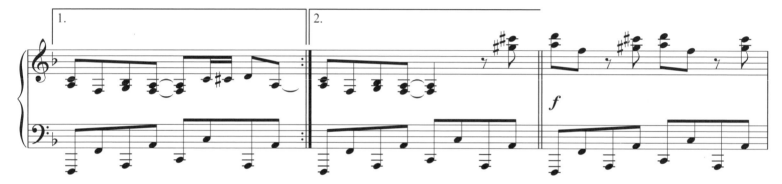

HONKY TONK TRAIN
(Honky Tonk Train Blues)

By MEADE "LUX" LEWIS

KAYCEE ON MY MIND

By PETE JOHNSON

Arrangement based on one by Pete Johnson

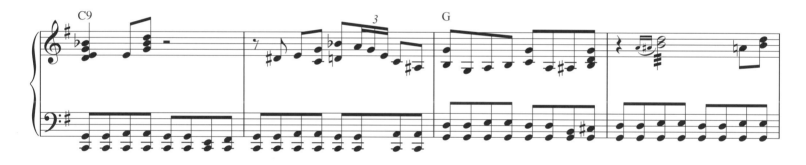

59

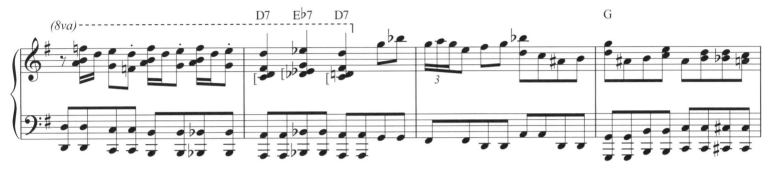

LET 'EM JUMP

By PETE JOHNSON

Bright Boogie Woogie, straight 8ths

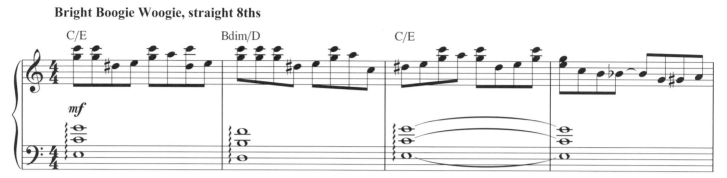

Arrangement based on one by Pete Johnson

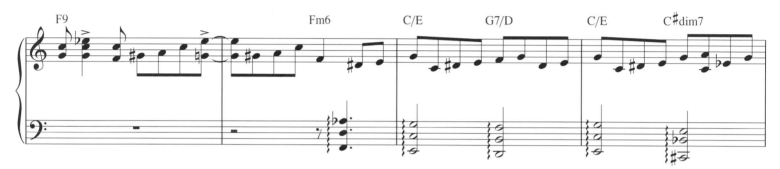

MESS AROUND

Words and Music by
AHMET ERTEGUN

Moderately fast, straight 8ths

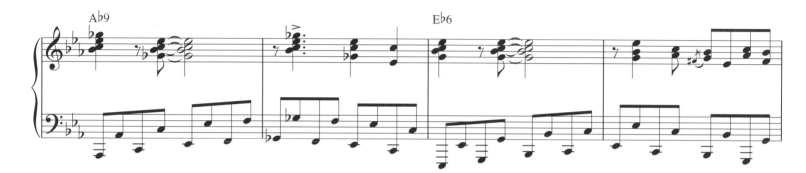

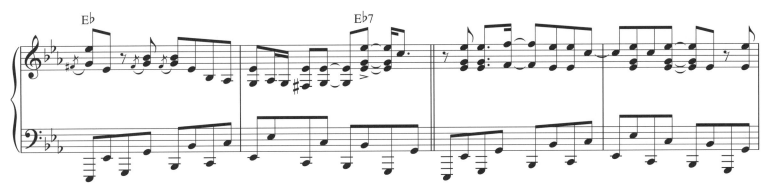

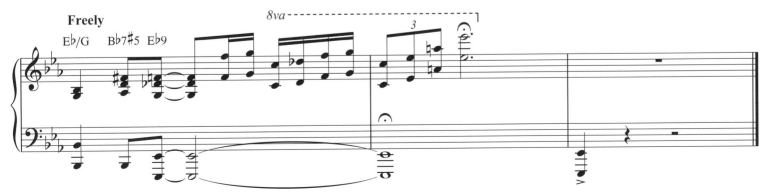

ST. LOUIS BLUES
from BIRTH OF THE BLUES

Words and Music by
W.C. HANDY

Moderately, with a Latin feel

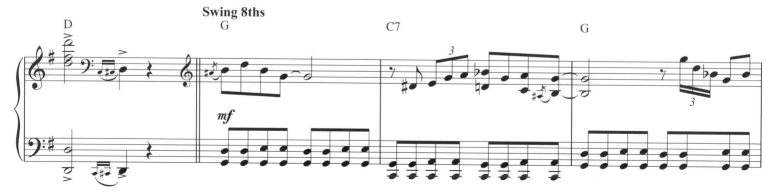

With a Latin feel

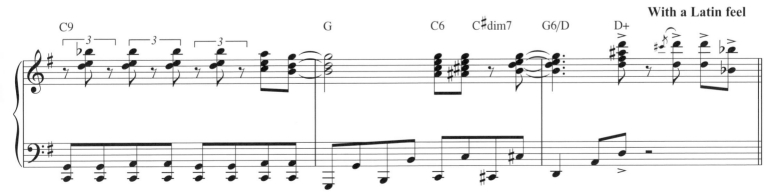

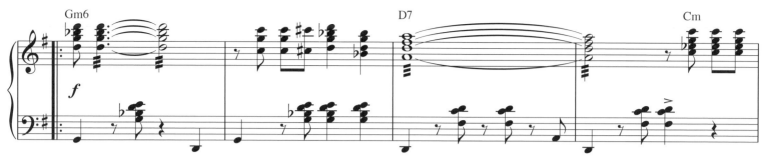

71

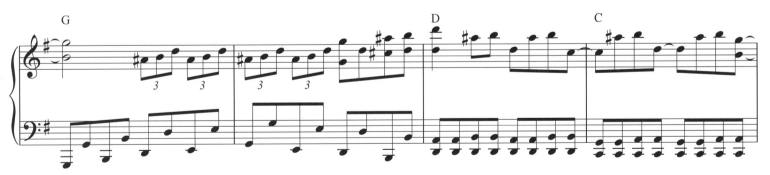

STATE STREET SPECIAL

Words and Music by
JAMES YANCEY

Moderate Swing

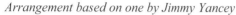

Arrangement based on one by Jimmy Yancey

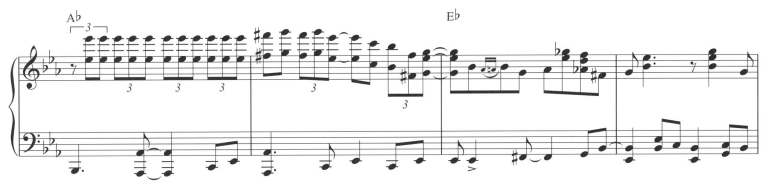

74

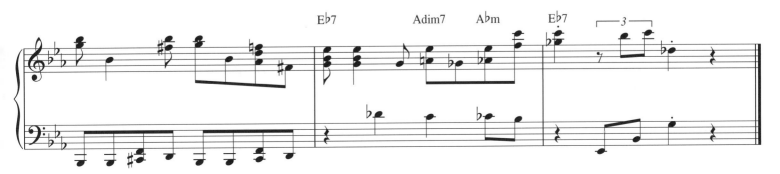

SUITCASE BLUES

By ALBERT AMMONS

Moderately slow Swing

Arrangement based on a performance by Albert Ammons

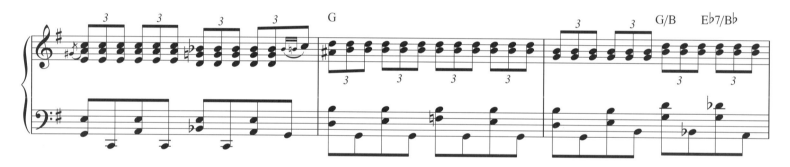

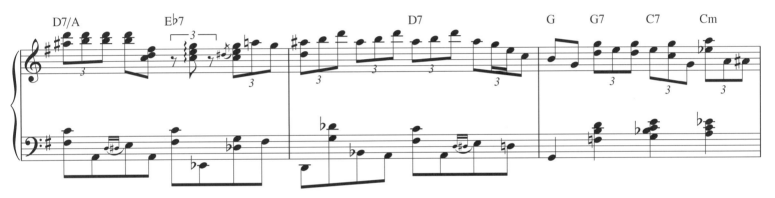

78

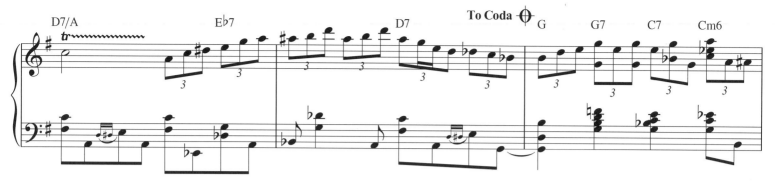

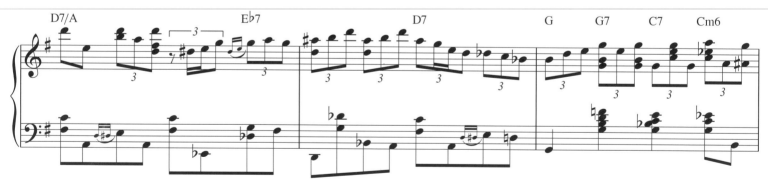

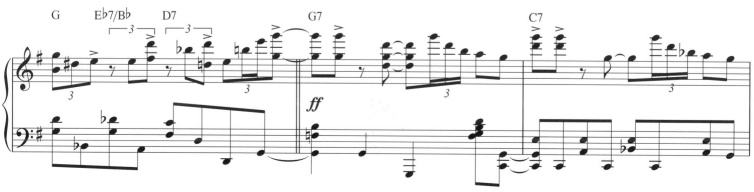

SWANEE RIVER BOOGIE

Music by HATTIE YOUNG

Moderately fast Swing

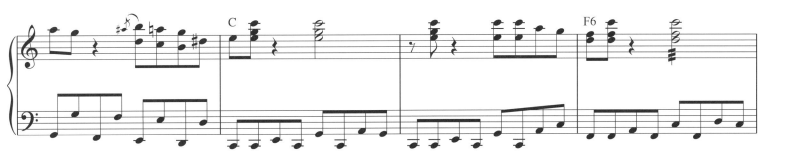

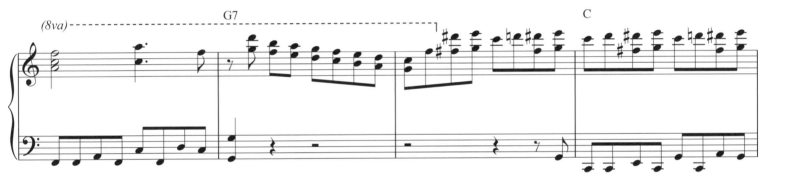

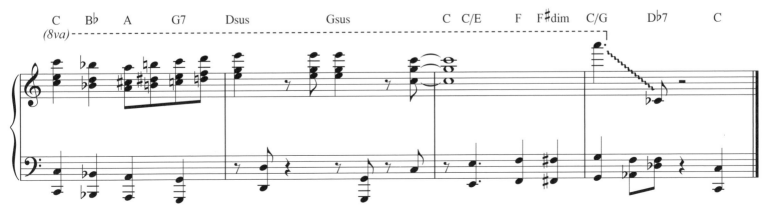

YANCEY SPECIAL

By MEADE "LUX" LEWIS

Moderate Swing

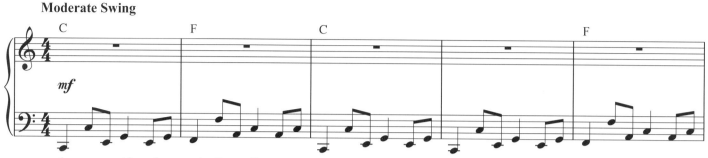

Arrangement based on one by Jimmy Yancey

86

SIXTH AVE EXPRESS

Words and Music by PETE JOHNSON
and ALBERT AMMONS

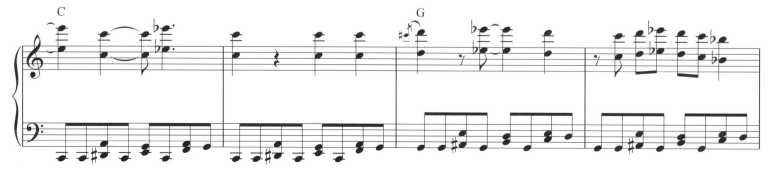

F   C

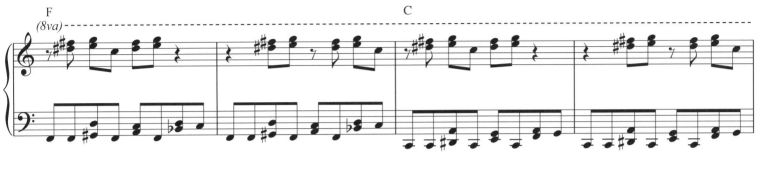

G7   C

F   C

G   C

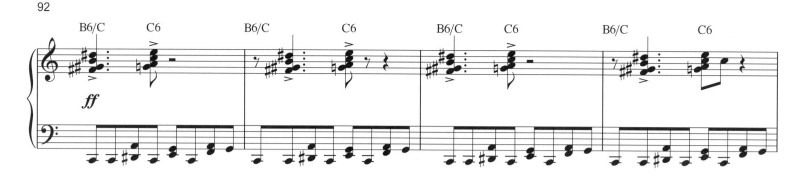

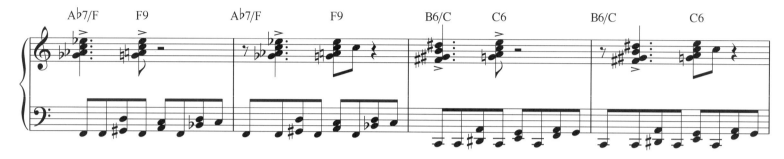

REAL BOOKS
Now Available in Your Favorite Styles of Music!

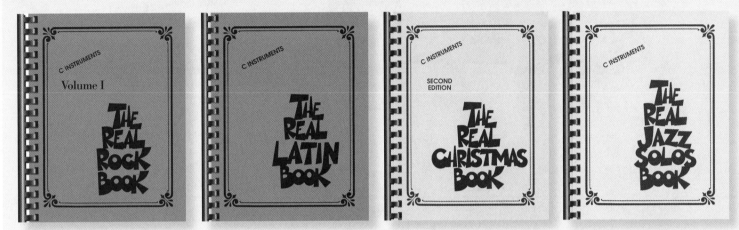

The Real Books are the best-selling jazz books of all time. Since the 1970s, musicians have trusted these volumes to get them through every gig, night after night. The problem is that the books were illegally produced and distributed, without any regard to copyright law, or royalties paid to the composers who created these musical masterpieces. Hal Leonard is very proud to present the first legitimate and legal editions of these books ever produced – and now has also published brand new volumes with a blockbuster selection of songs in a variety of genres.

Also available:

00295069	The Real Bebop Book E♭ Edition	$34.99
00154230	The Real Bebop Book C Edition	$34.99
00295068	The Real Bebop Book B♭ Edition	$34.99
00240264	The Real Blues Book	$34.99
00310910	The Real Bluegrass Book	$35.00
00240223	The Real Broadway Book	$35.00
00125426	The Real Country Book	$39.99
00240355	The Real Dixieland Book C Edition	$32.50
00122335	The Real Dixieland Book B♭ Edition	$35.00
00294853	The Real Dixieland Book E♭ Edition	$35.00
00240268	The Real Jazz Solos Book	$30.00
00240348	The Real Latin Book C Edition	$37.50
00127107	The Real Latin Book B♭ Edition	$35.00
00118324	The Real Pop Book – Vol. 1	$35.00
00295066	The Real Pop Book Vol. 1 B♭ Edition	$35.00
00286451	The Real Pop Book - Vol. 2	$35.00
00240437	The Real R&B Book C Edition	$39.99
00276590	The Real R&B Book B♭ Edition	$39.99
00240313	The Real Rock Book	$35.00
00240323	The Real Rock Book – Vol. 2	$35.00
00240359	The Real Tab Book	$32.50
00240317	The Real Worship Book	$29.99

THE REAL CHRISTMAS BOOK

00240306	C Edition	$35.00
00240345	B♭ Edition	$32.50
00240346	E♭ Edition	$35.00
00240347	Bass Clef Edition	$35.00
00240431	A-G CD Backing Tracks	$24.99
00240432	H-M CD Backing Tracks	$24.99
00240433	N-Y CD Backing Tracks	$24.99

HAL•LEONARD®
Complete song lists online at
www.halleonard.com

Prices, content, and availability subject to change without notice.

THE REAL BOOK MULTI-TRACKS

1. MAIDEN VOYAGE PLAY-ALONG

Autumn Leaves • Blue Bossa • Doxy • Footprints • Maiden Voyage • Now's the Time • On Green Dolphin Street • Satin Doll • Summertime • Tune Up.
00196616 Book with Online Media..........$17.99

2. MILES DAVIS PLAY-ALONG

Blue in Green • Boplicity (Be Bop Lives) • Four • Freddie Freeloader • Milestones • Nardis • Seven Steps to Heaven • So What • Solar • Walkin'.
00196798 Book with Online Media $17.99

3. ALL BLUES PLAY-ALONG

All Blues • Back at the Chicken Shack • Billie's Bounce (Bill's Bounce) • Birk's Works • Blues by Five • C-Jam Blues • Mr. P.C. • One for Daddy-O • Reunion Blues • Turnaround.
00196692 Book with Online Media $17.99

4. CHARLIE PARKER PLAY-ALONG

Anthropology • Blues for Alice • Confirmation • Donna Lee • K.C. Blues • Moose the Mooche • My Little Suede Shoes • Ornithology • Scrapple from the Apple • Yardbird Suite.
00196799 Book with Online Media $17.99

5. JAZZ FUNK PLAY-ALONG

Alligator Bogaloo • The Chicken • Cissy Strut • Cold Duck Time • Comin' Home Baby • Mercy, Mercy, Mercy • Put It Where You Want It • Sidewinder • Tom Cat • Watermelon Man.
00196728 Book with Online Media $17.99

6. SONNY ROLLINS PLAY-ALONG

Airegin • Blue Seven • Doxy • Duke of Iron • Oleo • Pent up House • St. Thomas • Sonnymoon for Two • Strode Rode • Tenor Madness.
00218264 Book with Online Media $17.99

7. THELONIOUS MONK PLAY-ALONG

Bemsha Swing • Blue Monk • Bright Mississippi • Green Chimneys • Monk's Dream • Reflections • Rhythm-a-ning • 'Round Midnight • Straight No Chaser • Ugly Beauty.
00232768 Book with Online Media $17.99

8. BEBOP ERA PLAY-ALONG

Au Privave • Boneology • Bouncing with Bud • Dexterity • Groovin' High • Half Nelson • In Walked Bud • Lady Bird • Move • Witches Pit.
00196728 Book with Online Media $17.99

9. CHRISTMAS CLASSICS PLAY-ALONG

Blue Christmas • Christmas Time Is Here • Frosty the Snow Man • Have Yourself a Merry Little Christmas • I'll Be Home for Christmas • My Favorite Things • Santa Claus Is Comin' to Town • Silver Bells • White Christmas • Winter Wonderland.
00236808 Book with Online Media..........$17.99

10. CHRISTMAS SONGS PLAY-ALONG

Away in a Manger • The First Noel • Go, Tell It on the Mountain • Hark! the Herald Angels Sing • Jingle Bells • Joy to the World • O Come, All Ye Faithful • O Holy Night • Up on the Housetop • We Wish You a Merry Christmas.
00236809 Book with Online Media..........$17.99

11. JOHN COLTRANE PLAY-ALONG

Blue Train (Blue Trane) • Central Park West • Cousin Mary • Giant Steps • Impressions • Lazy Bird • Moment's Notice • My Favorite Things • Naima (Niema) • Syeeda's Song Flute.
00275624 Book with Online Media $17.99

12. 1950S JAZZ PLAY-ALONG

Con Alma • Django • Doodlin' • In Your Own Sweet Way • Jeru • Jordu • Killer Joe • Lullaby of Birdland • Night Train • Waltz for Debby.
00275647 Book with Online Media $17.99

13. 1960S JAZZ PLAY-ALONG

Ceora • Dat Dere • Dolphin Dance • Equinox • Jeannine • Recorda Me • Stolen Moments • Tom Thumb • Up Jumped Spring • Windows.
00275651 Book with Online Media $17.99

14. 1970S JAZZ PLAY-ALONG

Birdland • Bolivia • Chameleon • 500 Miles High • Lucky Southern • Phase Dance • Red Baron • Red Clay • Spain • Sugar.
00275652 Book with Online Media $17.99

15. CHRISTMAS TUNES PLAY-ALONG

The Christmas Song (Chestnuts Roasting on an Open Fire) • Do You Hear What I Hear • Feliz Navidad • Here Comes Santa Claus (Right down Santa Claus Lane) • A Holly Jolly Christmas • Let It Snow! Let It Snow! Let It Snow! • The Little Drummer Boy • The Most Wonderful Time of the Year • Rudolph the Red-Nosed Reindeer • Sleigh Ride.
00278073 Book with Online Media $17.99